T0097879

Skywriting

Skywriting

AND OTHER POEMS

Charles Tomlinson

WINNER OF THE NEW CRITERION POETRY PRIZE

Ivan R. Dee

CHICAGO 2003

To Brenda

Library of Congress Cataloging-in-Publication Data:
Tomlinson, Charles, 1927–
    Skywriting : and other poems / Charles Tomlinson.
        p. cm.
    "Winner of the New Criterion Poetry Prize."
    ISBN 1-56663-541-1 (alk. paper)
        I. Title.

PR6039.O349S57 2003
821'.914—dc22   2003055504

Acknowledgments

Acknowledgments are due to the editors of the following: *Anterem*, *The Critical Quarterly*, *Last Words*, *Literary Imagination*, *The Times Literary Supplement*, *The New Criterion*, *Poetry Nation*, *La Stampa*. These poems first appeared in *The Hudson Review*: "Skywriting," "A Fragment from Mexico," "July on the High Plain."

Contents

I

Skywriting   *9*
Mexico: A Sequence   *11*
A Visit to Don Miguel   *21*
Waiting for the Bus at Tlacochahuaya   *23*
A Fragment from Mexico   *26*

II

From the Plane   *29*
Piazza   *30*
In Ferrara   *31*
The Etruscan Graveyard at Marzabotto   *32*
The Runners at San Benedetto   *34*
In June   *36*
July on the High Plain   *38*
The Journey: Pescocostanzo — Roma   *39*
Roma   *40*
Piazza Navona   *43*
Farewell to Europa   *45*

III

Japanese Notebook   *49*

To Shizue   52
For Nōrikō   53
Macao   54
On Lantau Island   56

IV

Waiting for John   59
Bristol Night Walk   60
Death of a Poet   62
For T. H.   64
Cotswold Journey (2001)   65
Spem in Alium   67
Trout   69
Track   70
Slow Down   71
Newark Park (an upward glance)   72
Reflection   74
In the Hallway   75
The Even Numbers   77
If Bach had been a Beekeeper   78
Midwinter   79
February   81
The Transformation   82
Ode to Memory   83
The Leaper   85
Fire and Air   87
Primal Fire   89
Watching Water   90
Floodtime   91
The Martins   92
Tonight   93

I

Skywriting

Three jets are streaking west:
   Trails are beginning to fray already:
The third, the last set out,
   Climbs parallel a March sky
Paying out a ruled white line:
   Skywriting like an incision,
Such surgical precision defines
   The mile between it and the others
Who have disappeared leaving behind
   Only their now ghostly tracks
That still hold to the height and map
   Their direction with a failing clarity:
The sky is higher for their passing
   Where the third plane scans its breadth.
The mere bare blue would never have shown
   That vaultlike curvature overhead,
Already evading the mathematics of the spot,
   As it blooms back, a cool canopy,
A celestial meadow, needing no measure
   But a reconnaissant eye, an ear

Aware suddenly that as they passed
    No sound accompanied arrival or vanishing
So high were their flight-paths on a sky
    That has gone on expunging them since,
Leaving a clean page there for chance
    To spread wide its unravelling hieroglyphs.

Mexico: A Sequence

I *Mexico*

It begins with the Atlantic from above:
   Far-down glimmerings of white on blue—
Blue that seemed all sky, but is betrayed
   Into revealing itself as sea, faintest
Dawnings of a pattern on the waves, white points
   As sharp as stars suddenly created, fading out:
A wave-capped ocean is what we glimpse
   Until blue takes over once again
As we keep trying to put together
   This wide ambiguity of air and water,
Cosmic theatre we cannot act in.
   Canada lies below, an open map,
A lesson in geography for us scholars
   Who imagine the route to Mexico must lie
Due south, not through dogged unfinished winter.
   Roads are crossing that map beside an estuary
Snow-beached, an island in it
   Rising patterned in snowy lozenges
Like the Inuit diagram of a fish. On shore
   Someone must have surveyed the place

And squared it off, leaving those lines
    As taut as wire to wait out winter
And surface through the snow, demarcations of nowhere.
    Only the lakes, with scratches on their ice
Like the tracks of skaters, seem to know
    Of the possibility of circles, of ellipses. Faced
By such evidence, shall we believe at last
    That this is spring, is south, is Mexico?

Entering the Doric nave, you might have thought
They were about to paint the entire interior,
But that iron corset of scaffolding was there
Literally to keep the cathedral on its feet.

The walls were collapsing, splaying outwards
While its innards were being penetrated
By the tip of Moctezuma's pyramid
Over which it had been built, prising it apart.

We got back to the car and the six-lane throroughfare
Out beyond Tacubaya where a gigantic Mexican flag
Failed to unfurl. Only the billboards went on storming the sky
Like trees in a tropical forest fighting for light.

At an intersection someone with a clown's white face
Rushed out grasping a step-ladder, mounted it
And began to juggle in mid-air a handful of balls.
This was one of the city's more inventive beggars.

A genuine artist, he was too slow in getting down
To claim the money we were holding ready for him
And escaped as the traffic surged only because of that nimbleness
Which gave his unpaid audacity such style.

There is a plan to bring back the lakes and the canals
Of the Aztec city, to irrigate once more the friable earth
And get rid of the cars. The beautiful idea
Hangs in the air like that unfluttering ensign.

At sundown the metropolis grows grateful to the eye
When the lights come on and it is their constellation confronts us,
And the ghosts of the fallen jacaranda blossoms
Drift smokily over the ground the colour of English bluebells.

III *Xochimilco*

With its network of canals and its artificial islands, Xochimilco is the location from which Cortés in 1519 advanced on Tenochtitlán, the site of Mexico City.

1. *Isste*

Clerks, on holiday,
navigate at leisure
the waters of this moated fortress
time has turned into a pleasure garden.
Bannered above them looms
their sibillant acronym *Isste*—
Instituto de Seguridad Social
al Servicio de los Trabajadores
del Estado: Isste
which seems in tune
with the sound of water
the pole of the remero lifts
along a shore whose intersecting twigs
hold floating islands together
that have taken root. All
are free today
to sway in unison,
while the two waltzing
so chastely in the narrow bows
seem to dance
almost without movement:
mariachi at the prow
trumpet the excursionists' approach
while in the stern guitars
and a violin thrum a passage through
the diminished empire of these isles
from which the exasperated conquistador

combed out their ancestors.

2. *Marimba*

The two marimberos confront
their instrument, this
Kaffir piano that the slave trade
brought to these shores: a prelusive
quivering of wooden keys,
a ripple of sound shadows
over the buzz of bass: their steersman
slides them in close beside our boat,
holding them steady there.
What water music will they float out now?
They suggest items like knowledgeable waiters
when one hesitates
toying with the menu—La Zandunga?—
and bring down drumsticks
selecting notes
for this dance of dignity. The elate
vibration takes fire but never conflagrates,
holding a dulcet truce
while in full flow
like the channel we ride on.
Or Las Chiapanecas?—
the beat is no burden
to this swifter sweetness.
The others I forget, recall
only a different kind of note,
the flicker of paper pesos
fluttering thanks and encouragement, as we
enter this causeway crowded with gondoliers
whose accuracy is the guarantee

of our own safe circuit
back to the embarcadero and the quay.

3. *Words*

Under his awning,
Cernuda visited this spot.
He heard only echoes
of extinct wisdom, of abdicated life.
Silent figures held out a flower, a fruit
from their passing boats
and evidently knew the secret of it all
but did not reveal it.
A veiled sky darkened the waters,
the poplars took on a sickly look,
the musicians seemed to have grown old.
Under funereal branches, he saw
the boats of the sellers of flowers
venture out
to pay periodic tribute
to their drowned recollection of the place,
webbed them in words
and relished that bitter satisfaction
flooding tongue and pen.
Today asks no more
to disperse the Klingsor spell and curse
that words can cast over things
than the sweet acridity
drifting across the sense
where a pair of vendors bend
at their brazier roasting maize,
while, on the bank above,
a knock-kneed foal

a branch between its teeth,
is chewing on leaves as new-born as itself,
cantering into view
as if it were the smoke-smell
had woken it to life
and the sky behind it and beyond might well
revive those distinctnesses of line and hue
that, once, in the rarified air,
seemed to annihilate distance.

[Section 3 contains a paraphrase of Cernuda's prose
poem, "Por el Agua."]

After the fume of the streets, in front of the massive doors of Casa de Alvarado, Mexico itself—always a composite self—becomes palpable once more: the wall, painted dark red and patterned with lozenge-shapes of white stucco, is Moorish in style, *mudejar*. Like the doors it has an impregnable look. High above the doors a small, columned shrine, a saint inside, on top of the shrine a cross of that same ox-blood colour on a red ball laced round with a cross of white stucco. At the shrill bell, the doors are opened and one enters a courtyard sunk deep in time, whose shadows are as cool as a well. Pigeons fly down to drink at a circular, tiled basin of stone. From the level of the upper patio, a giant magnolia and bougainvilleas hang over. Through the shadowy recess of an archway light falls into a garden beyond, where tiny squirrels with serpentine tails move through the greenery like black weasels. Two eagles are visitors to the trees of this urban Eden.

For years the place was inhabited by an American woman, an archeologist. They say she was a sun-worshipper, but Lawrence who visited her here on three occasions, describes her as someone more dryly rational, "an odd number who could give the even numbers a bad time." Her black idols, baskets and shields have been long swept away.

But who was Alvarado? They say he was one of Cortés' captains, the same Alvarado the Aztecs thought of as kin to the sun-god because of his red hair and called him Tonatio or Son of the Sun. It was he who performed the famous jump—el salto de Alvarado—when, surrounded by Aztec assailants in canoes and on land, he used his lance as a vaulting pole to leap over a canal and escape them.

Whether this is the true Alvarado of Casa de Alvarado, who can say with certainty? The history of the house and its garden must now also include that of Octavio Paz, the poet who came here to die and to seek, he said, reconciliation beneath these trees with their eagles and beside the cool basin frequented by pigeons. The house in Mixcoac, where he spent his childhood, is a convent. This house, where his days were to end, came nearest perhaps to the recollection of its garden and to that other garden in India where he was married beneath a giant neem tree, "above its shoulders, the sky with its barbarian jewels." The jewelled sky awaited him above this final garden which has survived the degradation of the City of Mexico, ravished almost as thoroughly as Aztec Tenochtitlán. "There are no gardens," he once wrote, "except those we carry with us." Here, a flat-topped arch opens in space another space, another time in time, the shade and shape of trees filling with their presences the garden into which this opening invites us. In the quiet of this sculpted clearing, we are standing in the middle of the world's biggest city that keeps moving, without pause or limit, out over the levels of the Valley of Mexico like lava.

A Visit to Don Miguel

I am about to leave
when he tells me: "Five
of the president's bodyguard
have been shot dead." "Strange.
Nothing about it in the press."
"There won't be. My brother telephoned
with the news. They will never
confess that it happened. You like this house?
It's haunted. One day
our maid saw a ghost in the dining room.
When we rushed in, there was nothing there—
only the smell of a cigar
in a house where nobody smokes. Years ago
there were executions in the garden—
that's where the ghosts come from
through the back wall
where there's no entrance, you see." I see.

Then he suddenly adds:
"I've been temporarily retired
for political indiscretions.
I shall return to my post next year
provided I remain discreet." Outside the door,
"Perhaps discretion"—I put it to Roberto
who brought me here—"is not his strong suit?"
But there is almost pride in the reply.
"Miguel es un gran conversador."

Waiting for the Bus
at Tlacochahuaya

                    Goats
gnawing the prickly pears
with rock-hard jaws
lean between sand and spines
up into the bush. The crossroads
grow festive as we wait:
it is a subdued festivity
when the people of two villages
meet at a crossroads and kiss hands,
gathering into both their own
the hand to be kissed and with warmth
kiss it, saying softly
Qué tal? Qué tal? The surprise
is a ritual surprise—
not so that of the two young men
who know each other yet did not know
both were travelling today
and to the same place—*Aah!*—
and having patted each other
they embrace, wandering side by side
absorbed in the fact of friendship.

A man leads three bulls
across the road, but no one
takes this in: they have eyes
only for humanity—the goats
are also invisible to them.
When we entered the village
a man on a burro had saluted us:
You are going to Tlacochahuaya?
We moved on through the *Buenos días*
of others and to the church
where a one-armed Indian
stood at the door and silent
gestured us inside, but this one-armed guide
neither guided nor begged.
Darkness, then the painted walls
covered with an angel army
—more cupids than angels:
the Dominicans had taught their flock
to paint them here
and unthrone Tlaloc (still tongued
in the village name)
and to convert the pagan gods
into saints and demons.
Two small girls followed us
as we left, asking
apologetically almost
for *moni, moni, moni,*
merely murmuring the word.
We regained the crossroads
and the man on the burro, returning,
was it stated or enquired
You have been to Tlacochahuaya?

And now out of the dust
a bus that will carry us back
suddenly arrives and the conductor
reciting *Oaxaca, Oaxaca,*
begins to stow aboard
his restive customers until
they fill the interior
and, giving blow on blow
to the resonant metal of the vehicle,
conveys to the waiting *operador*
it is time to go.

A Fragment from Mexico

Waiting in the sand, this
terracotta shard of a face
smiled on: when we
unearthed that smile
it did not anticipate the mile on mile
it must travel to here.
It is more leer than smile,
that almost lecherous anticipation
awaiting the sacrifice
when the sun-god is fed
on human hearts:
and still it awaits
and will outsmile
even the deaths of all the gods
under the wide grey of this sky.

II

From the Plane

for Kālmān Ruttkay

Ruskin would have seen a reason for flying
   On a day like this, with cloud shadows
Blown-by below, shaping out the land
   They clamber across—the immense
Body of Europe, with its mountains spread
   Beneath one's feet. One's feet? Why, they and we
Tread twenty thousand feet of space
   Between ourselves and the relief of Chamonix.
Yet from the ground, he could already see
   The hollow in the heart of the aiguille
As smooth and sweeping in its cavity
   As the curve of a vast oyster shell,
The connected movement in those crested masses
   Like that of sea waves, governed by
One under-sweep of tide that ran
   Through the whole body of the mountain chain.
Ruskin did not need to fly: his eye
   Flew for and back to him and what we see
At this height, he taught us standing on two feet,
   Among rocks the metallic tines of water
Curve across and down, into the course
   Of the hurrying river that uncoils its force
Tasselling-on to the unseen horizon.

Piazza

In the piazza at Ascoli Piceno
    The people walk on travertine, not asphalt—
Marble that paviours patterned into squares
    Each with its slim, stone borders
In a mathematic of recession. All the generations
    Go their measured way and savour now
The sharp air of a winter Sunday.
    That child, muffled against the cold,
Has discovered the long line of stone
    Slicing the centre of the expanse
And is following it, has to be restrained,
    Pacified, but already he has caught
A border stretching out edgeways,
    Sets off to follow that. One day
He will put it all together, time
    That he does not know exists, teaching him
To eye it all entire, admit
    That these leisurely restrictions are a fiction
That reveals the real, mapping our footfalls,
    Our swung arms, our slow dance here,
For an afternoon the guests of symmetry,
    Treading its stones in this theatre of chance.

In Ferrara

Carp the size of sheep
muscle their course to the surface
as they leap at the scraps of bread
flung their way. The concerted rush
raises a ripple, pushes back
the floating sediment
on this moat of the Estensi
and leaves a clear, clean space for play
over the beer-brown depths,
bellies glittering, disappearing.
It was energy like this
raised those walls, their height
filled with unfurnished emptiness now.
It is night. The street lamps
punctuate the alternation
of a depth-charge force and a dead calm
under this lavish scattering of bread.

The Etruscan Graveyard at Marzabotto

At the dump, the packaged waste
as neat as war-graves
awaits destruction:
the drone of a generator
insists on efficiency, promises
to destroy all traces:
on the spring wind
there is one other sound,
the whisper of discarded cellophane
like the voices of the dead
shiny and shivering with the season.
On the hill-top remain
in a fold of land
graves that are blocks of tufa,
the dark rock splashed
with ring on ring of orange
from the lichen
that thrives on nothing. One might choose

to lie here and be reclaimed by earth,
as clean as the emptiness
within each box of stone
that has no lid, but lies
open to the dateless sky
that has forgotten
how far their race once spread
who, dead, so succinctly occupy
so small a space.

The Runners at San Benedetto

Two runners are crossing the shore by night:
    Their sound on sand, their lithe iambics gauge
The certainty of arrival and return
    Before the wide encroachment of the waters
Smoothes out their footprint frontier. Cloud
    Keeps dulling the cusps of a moon
Just risen. A steadier glow
    From the endless necklace of the lungomare,
A fitful one from the circling beam
    Of a lighthouse that dapples keels
Close-packed, rocking at anchor.
    For lovers crossing the shore by night,
None of this is their concern. They see
    In the unpaved pathway a chosen destiny:
They choose each other and this place,
    Place to return to and by night re-pace
In the twilit ritual that runs between
    The competing geometries of shore and sky

Where the first stars prick their courses.
    Lovers, how many years of light
Await you behind that sky I cannot say:
    Your compact with the dark will guide you where
Beneath time's leisurely eye, the common day
    Tests this accord that was confirmed by night.

In June

In town today
wind and sunlight
investigated together
the costumes of passers-by
feeling and fluttering
the thin-spun stuffs
people put on in summer,
to find out whether they
belonged here or beyond, almost
painting them where they walked
or stood, constantly
re-shaping with billowing
brush-strokes, with free-hand
fantasies of a preliminary
sketch—preliminary that is
to further alterations, as if
unwilling to leave them
and their things

as now winged and now
shrunk back
into unchanging normality
only to take fire there
and swell out once again
from man to angel

July on the High Plain

Baled hay: the shaved land
   Where the cut crop grew and lay
Says that the multicoloured summer
   Is at an end. A pallid promontory
Extends between bare peaks,
   The roadside poplar rows
Crossing it at eccentric angles
   Beneath the bald crown of a mountain
Tonsured round by beeches. At noon
   Each tree sheds a shadow,
A perfect, separate circle on the ground,
   A dark disc one might well lift
And take away. But one must be swift
   Before the atmosphere consolidates as mist
And extinguishes all outline to become
   The black rainstains on every stone
In the evening storm, the downpour
   Babbling on the roof its liquid glossolalia,
As lightning explores the sleeping face of nature.

The Journey: Pescocostanzo—Roma

The tunnel-mouth irises-in
   Encircling and then lets go
The heights we enter, free to grow
   Now beyond us, to fall away below
Repeating the story of their making,
   As shapes come flowing into solidity,
Ranges re-group and stand
   Firm for as long as it takes an eye
To grasp them and the car flash by
   Into a new configuration. The next
Mouth issues us out over cloud—
   We are not rising, we are coming down
Through all these petrine metamorphoses
   To where the mist hangs low above Sulmona
In the gradual descent—the serrated mountains
   Soon behind us, the ramparts raising
On stone hands walls, houses, towers
   Towards eventual snow—down
To the lesser slopes, the Roman seven,
   As slowly the vines climb back across the land.

[Sulmona was the birthplace of Ovid.]

Roma

I *Monte del Gallo*

The faintest breeze is stirring finger-fronds
Of the many-fingered hands that seem to stroke
The inaudible keyboard that is air:
The raised draped pine-boughs float on tides unseen
That lift then let them go, submerged
In the impersonality of trunks. Two cypresses
Grown close together, leaned on by the wind,
Seem to acknowledge one another's presence—
Human, would be moving to an embrace—
But they, too, like the sea-beast pines, submit
To the oceanic motion parting them,
Provoking us with their silences, their deep
Arboreal indifference to unsleeping Rome.

II *At Tivoli*

Did Hadrian bring Antinous his friend
To hear the nightingales beside this pool
On summer afternoons? They sing today
As though the centuries had done no harm
To one's authority and the other's charm
And we might find them here between these walls
Of what was once a palace and retreat
Built for the pleasure of the senses where
One naked headless athlete poses still
Reflected by the water. In the sun,
Drowning the crickets in the dusty grass,
The unquenchable loud nightingales flow on.

III *Liszt at the Villa D'Este*

How liquidly he matches cadences
Against suggestions that the lilt of water
Raises in his mind. The deliquescence
Still runs pure across the barlines of the score,
But under the centennial cypress trees
No shaping hand can purify this rush
Of currents you must neither touch nor taste
Laced with contaminations from a land turned waste.

IV *In the Park*

In the park, a deserted carousel,
The *padrona* sits behind her newspaper.
Riderless the animals do not stir,
Then rock, half-restive, as traffic moves the air.

Two piebalds with a coach, an elephant,
A miniature house, a castle keep—
You could imagine them circling from their sleep
Awakened by wheezing music. I write it down

The childless silence, the animals of wood
Glittering, new painted and unreal—
The prince's playthings left beneath the trees;
Quiet axle of the city's turning wheel.

But the woman's face rises above the pages:
Che fa, signore? She takes me for some spy
Inspecting the safety of her paradise.
Scrivo una poesia, I reply.

Half convinced, she shifts from foot to foot
While she persuades herself. *Bene*, she says
At last, subsides once more beneath her sheets,
Invisible as the stanza's lock clicks shut.

Piazza Navona

The pigeons
make a moveable feast
for the leisured eye,
crowning the sculpture round the fountain: one
sits on the head of a cupid,
one on his wing,
another astride the back
of a petrified crab whose claws
steady it against the brow of a triton
mouthing a water-jet
out of a seaweed-bearded
gap-toothed aperture
that grimaces pain: cupid
is indifferent to this
as he crawls towards the crab
but cannot take hold

because of the intervening pigeon
riding its carapace: his expression
—all interest and anxiety
to achieve his end—appears
to take in the unlooked-for
but now perceived obstruction,
and you might almost swear
a flash of infantile frustration
was dawning on his face: all this
in detail from a time
when architecture, too,
was one of the arts of decoration.

Farewell to Europa

Europa
carried away astride the back
of a motorcycle, horns
and handlebars make a fair match,
but this bride of the machine,
having lost her head,
shows no more now
than the disc of a breast,
an echo of the wheels,
hubbed by its nipple.
Speed has cancelled her out and she
is pleased to be no more
than this faceless rhyme in space
which cannot even see
the landscape of her future
rolling towards her
through the sodium glow
of dismantled towns.

III

Japanese Notebook

The falling blossom
I saw drift back to the branch
was a butterfly.
—Moritake

for Takashi Tsujii

The circular window
(unglazed)
in the shrine at Kamakura
borrows the landscape and transforms it
into a roundel on the wall

The rice grains
in the porcelain
of the teacup
let through light

Bridge of a spider's web
leaves resting on it
as on the telephone wires
above the bamboo grove

Legs of the spider
half-way between
the shambling of a crab
and the parrot's claw
scaling the wires of its cage
in laborious methodical ascent

Immense wooden temples
that look like celestial barns
full of invisible grain

Fat ropes of straw
embrace and sanctify
the trunks of the ancient pines
that climb so high
before their foliage begins

A tree mummified in bandages
it has been there seven-hundred years
and must be fortified
against the diseases of old age

A bamboo pipe drips
dropping condensation
from rocks into a well
already overflowing

The falling leaf
that turns out not to be
Moritake's butterfly
has reached the ground

Bashō's cicada drills no rocks
but emerges from the dust
a tarnished link
in the foodchain of the ants
lifting it by its feelers

Clouds
that keep removing
the miniature mountains of Izu
have abolished Fuji

To Shizue

They tell me
"quiet bough"
is the meaning of your name.
Who now
will uncomplainingly accept
the given air? —
it was not this
they wanted, but the lurch
and wave-lash
of infinite variety:
too few will thank you
for the calm
your name contains
that, bearing fruit,
has no need
to greedily call out
for what is not here,
but lets the bough
ride the stir
on the scarcely
undulated atmosphere.

For Nōrikō

Seeing the blossoms on our cherry tree,
I thought of the strokes of your calligraphy
Riding on the air that was the page
Your brush was hovering over: stage by stage
A sudden blossoming of each character,
Of living letters, sprung from nowhere,
As though the sheet were both the bough and air.
If, in all this, your writing seemed a tree
Putting forth petals, what of your artistry,
How many centuries flowing through that arm?
One might have sworn each rapid touch was warm
With the life that was in you and others;
The brushwork at an end, the text still stirs
In this undecided light, this hesitating
English winter half-arrived at spring.

Macao

Banyans
spilling Spanish moss
shade a park. A fragment
of Catholic Europe—a church front:
the drift and perfume of joss
invade the missing nave
from the shrine beneath it. The library
vanished in fire like the nave itself,
neither to be restored. A cat
sits in the threshold dust
of the Pagoda da Barra, its kittens
asleep by the altar.
In the protestant church
the basket-work pews
are painted brown
to resemble mahogany:
in its graveyard lies
the apprentice boy "who died on board
of a fall into the hold."   It is four o'clock
in the world of time
through which pour
schoolchildren in blazers
past a bust of Da Gama

greening on its marble plinth.
Smouldering overhead,
feeding the temple haze,
hang the coils of joss
that soil with dropped ash
the stone bed
where bundles of dozing fur
do not stir below
those cigarettes of eternity.

On Lantau Island

A dog-pack circles the monastery grounds:
in the shade of its boundary wall
they take their rest, exuding an odour
like pungent tweed. The testier dogs
still snarl at one another. Leadership
or plain dislike puts them on edge
spikily vulnerable. Then they are off
and some collective impulse, subliminal sense of lack
steers them elsewhere: the ill tempered
defer their resentments, mounted and unfulfilled
the copulatory lose balance, dragged
rolling apart into the spate of general will.
The tide washes on and subsides by the gate.
Heave and relapse, and the bickerings begin again.
Who reincarnated in them? They will be joined one day
by the nun reciting her scriptures sotto voce
who forfeits nirvana by periodically
baring her teeth and screaming
at the unbiddable tourists who insist
on photographing the gods of the temple annex:
in their lotus thrones the three gold buddhas
float weightlessly, buoyed up like the boats
that carried them here through the uncertain sea.

IV

Waiting for John

The trains that day were running late.
  Near the station, swayed a stand of pines
Like a group of stranded travellers
  That had taken root. Suddenly
The wind passed through and drew from them
  A noise like a train arriving—though
After the windy onset, nothing occurred
  Except more such imitations. Bemused, I hailed the thought
Of a form of transport more than terrestrial
  In the alternation overhead of sound and silence,
In the battery of breeze among resonant treetops.
  But how quiet reality is, sliding into its berth,
And the twelve thirty-four arriving on earth
  Modestly filled up space under the roar of boughs.
I missed the hiss of doors opening, the clatter of feet.
  I had come merely to meet someone.
Had I been travelling, I would not have caught
  That stealthy arrival while staring at the trees.
But something caused me to turn and recognise
  An approaching face, good to see
After time's long gap. Let me take your case.
  What sounds were those that followed us from there?
Was it the rage of pines or a train's departure?

Bristol Night Walk

It is not far—
Given the mind's propensity to travel
And not leave the spot. Morse
From the Cabot Tower is signaling our existence
To Mars, and though there is no one there
To appreciate the clair de terre, the pulse
Of light at the bottom of this well,
You face all that emptiness overhead
With equanimity, the city spread before you—
So much movement round fixed points,
Spire, tower and bridge. The dew
Of this warm night will leave each statue
Drenched and shining. But not yet.
They loom now in nocturnal gravity—
Burke advancing behind the gesture of his hand,
And through the traffic fume the horse
Bearing royal William, stretches wide
Nostrils that look as though they scent it.

The dew is gathering under darkness,
    Glistening in silence where the bridge
Leaps the vacancy of the abyss it spans:
    We hang here balanced between iron and stone
Under the equilibrium of such stars
    As prick the vault above us, our fragility
For the moment shielded in the palm of space.

Death of a Poet

i.m. Ted Hughes

It was a death that brought us south,
    Along a roadway that did not exist
When the friendship was beginning death has ended.
    How lightly, now, death leans
Above the counties and the goings-on
    Of loud arterial England. I see
A man emerge out of a tent,
    Pitched at a field's edge, his back
Towards the traffic, taking in
    The flat expanse of Sedgemoor, as if history
Had not occurred, the drumming tyres
    Creating one wide silence.
Oaks stand beside their early shadows.
    Sun makes of a man's two shadow-legs
Long blades for scissoring the way
    Across yet one more meadow, shortening it.
Hardy's rivers—Parrett, Yeo, Tone—
    Flash flood waters at us. Then,
As the flatlands cede to patchwork Devon,
    Again you cannot quite foretell the way

Dartmoor will rise up behind its mists,
    As solid as they are shifting. Sun,
Without warning, sets alight the fields,
    In anticipation of that other unison
As fire enters body, body fire,
    And every lineament gone, dissolves
The seal and simplification of human limits.
    Mourners drift out of the church,
Stand watching the slow cortège
    Of car and hearse wind through the street
To that last unmaking. The net of lanes
    Entangles our departure, hedges
Zapped spruce against the expectation
    Of another spring. Scarcely time
To recall the lanes we walked in or the coast
    That heard our midland and his northern voice
Against a wind that snatched their sounds.
    The small hawks caught the light
Below us, crossing the Hartland bays
    Over endless metamorphoses of water.
Voice-prints, like foot-prints, disappear
    But sooner; though more lingeringly
They go on fading in the ear.
    We join the highway that is England now.
The moon, a thin bronze mirror
    Reflecting nothing, a rush of cloud
Suddenly effaces. The line of oaks
    That at morning stood beside their shadows
Are the shades themselves on our return.

For T. H.

I caught today something that you'd once said.
It re-formed in the echo-chambers of the head
Bringing with it the voice of its saying
(Your voice) and even the atmosphere of a morning
On Hartland's cliffs and the steady pace that we
Kept up beside the murmurings of that sea.
It was the music of speech you were describing
And the way such sounds must either die or sing,
The satisfactions of speech being musical
When we talk together: a man with no talent at all
For music in the matters of everyday
Stays tedious despite what he has to say—
Even on subjects that might wake one's fantasies,
For what we want is that exchange of melodies,
The stimulation of tunes that answer one another
In the salt and sway of the sea's own weather
As they did that day we faced into the wind there,
And now return in thought, so that I hear
The dance of the words, like verse itself, renew
The sounded lineaments of the world we move through.

Cotswold Journey (2001)

A day before the war and driving east,
　　We catch the rasp of ignited engines —
Planes practising combat above this shire
　　Of Norman masonry, limestone walls.
In their quiet, they seemed so permanent
　　Under the changing light. But the tower
We stand beneath is hacked by sound
　　Out of the centuries it has inhabited
With such certainty. After the flash
　　We stand once more on stable ground
Under chevroned arches, climb the stair
　　Up to the dovecot where the priest
Once fetched the victims down that he would eat.
　　The form remains, the victims have all gone
From nesting places squared in stone,
　　Boxes of empty darkness now. The planes streak on
Returning out of the unsteady brightness,
　　The blue that rain could smear away
But does not. Sun turns into silhouettes
　　The gargoyles clinging to sheer surfaces
That rise above us. Sun travels beside us
　　As we penetrate deeper in, lose track

Of the plane-ways that leave no vapour trails
    To decorate their passage through
In abstract fury. Courteous walls
    Rise out of stone-crowned summits,
Prelude and then surround a dwelling space
    With church and inn — for us the solace
Of a now twilit afternoon. We explore
    Before we eat, the inn-yard and the street beyond,
Where Saxon masons, raising arch and jamb,
    Cut leaves of acanthus whose weathered surfaces
Hold onto fragile form. The night
    Slowly extinguishes their edges but bequeaths
To the mind the lasting glimmer still
    Of stone come to life. The inn
Recalls us through the village street
    And I remember how a friend once said,
Speaking with a Yorkshireman's conciseness,
    "A native gift for townscape, a parochialism
But of a Tuscan kind." Our return
    Is silent although we travel by
Lanes tracing the outlines of the airbase
    And, there, all we manage to decipher
Is the gleam of wired restriction, barbs
    That bar us out from sterile acres
Awaiting the future in a moonless quiet.
    Rain, with the clink of the lifted latch
On our arrival, bursts from the darkness where
    East and west, preparing to unseam
The sleeping world below that height,
    Downpour drops its curtain on the past
And the cry of the muezzin infiltrates first light.

Spem in Alium

I have placed my hope in no other god but thee,
Transfiguring spirit of poetry,
And as the levels of the landscape rise
In roofline, tree and hill before my eyes,
Until the clouds themselves are earthed in light,
Their changes show the world is not complete
And never will be, as we read its book,
Transfiguration glancing with each look,
Whenever light (changing itself) descries
Another variation for the eyes,
All climbing like a counterpoint of voices,
And sight aware of what, unsighted, stays
Hidden behind a foreground and a meaning
Which cannot be restricted to the thing
Shorn of the spaces that surround its being.
Tallis, you tell the poet what is here
As if that arch of song which throngs the ear,
Shaping not only the invisible,
Rang like the currency of daylight, full
Of the nearby and the answering distances,

Outward and far to where the horizon lies:
And in the altered light there, you can weigh
The pull of the planet travelling its sky,
And one more journey to another day
Complete, and waiting on a dawn unseen,
Unhurriedly to let the changes re-begin.

[*Spem in Alium*: Tallis' motet for forty voices: "I have
never placed my hope in any other than thee…" (Spem in
alium nunquam habui praeter in te…).]

Trout

A trout, facing upstream, hangs
    Balanced against the current he is riding:
Tail and fins countervail the force
    Which keeps compelling him into acquiescence:
The delicate blades of his resistance
    Outflicker the ceaseless pouring of its course:
He has taken his stand midstream
    And will stay suspended there as long
As the need lasts in this unhurried hunt
    For what will feed him. It is attention
Steadies him within this element where
    Nothing is still, toning his faculties
To penetrate the twilight of its depths,
    Holding him poised until a darker shade
Falls across the flow and could presage his end:
    As swift as he was still, he backs with the current,
Glides beneath the bank, waits there,
    Meditates in the sliding gloom and lets
Death's trailing shadow slowly disappear
    Into the summer growth of one more year.

Track

Out of the wood, into the wood beyond
Trails flatten the grass between, and tell
Of midnight passages. These signs for silence
Dwell within the mind's own silences
Breeding a mystery—mysterious, too,
Even when explanation has restored it
To a world not shaped by introspection
And to lives lived-out beside our own
Nocturnal and unseen. Tracing a track
Badger or fox had smoothed, our glances fell
With the slope it followed, with a certainty
That taught us too, to see—sheer as it was—
The sure line of what accuracy aimed it
Through tunnelled tussocks, out beneath a fence
And down once more, a slither across marl,
To vertically reach the brink and bank
Where water, telling a story of its own,
Quarreling with the debris in its course,
Flashed with the light of early afternoon
That message, to be scented while we slept,
Of satisfaction to the ones who drink by night.

Slow
Down

it has warned all winter
at the blind corner as if
yes all two syllables
were needed to impress
the speeding eye. The advance
of March grass and of weed
has overshot from D to N
the bottom line by now
to show that yes a single
syllable will do the work of two
with that succinct sign
springing up out of leaves
like a growing thing.

Newark Park
(an upward glance)

i.m. Robert Parsons, Texan

Low winter sun,
as accurate as a gunsight,
aims all of its light
at the façade glass
that blinds and blazes
from the hill-top.
The wood that comes between
our eyes and it—
a black phalanx of winter trees—
puts out that brightness.
But among those trunks—
a hail of diamond,
comet train caught
through a drawn curtain.
Then the whole reflection
slides into sight once more.
"A lighthouse," I say, and you:
"More like a ship
leaning into view."
New ark, indeed,
ferrying toward the coast of evening

all those seeds of light,
all the energy futurity
cannot exhaust overnight.
The ship stands (it is darkening
along its decks)
in sight of the black coast
glimmering with frost—
cost of such clarity
as the January afternoon
brought to flare, higher and higher,
oxygen to that bonfire
now gone out.

Reflection

A reflection on the pane
has repositioned the chest of drawers
under the mahonia bush
on the lawn outside.
One drawer lies open to the rain
perfectly dry. Let the eye
follow that image
to where an interior door
cuts across the night,
as if there were many mansions to explore
under the gathered gloom,
room on room of them
in enfilade across the garden
left open to the coming generations
of this house already old.

In the Hallway

What I like in a house
is the room one cannot quite see—
the one with its door half-open,
showing a mere sliver of wall,
a picture sliced in half,
a mirror reflecting a window
that is invisible from outside
where you stand in the hallway
and the owner's lady
emerges from above, revealing
how intricate is the space up there
because of a landing which casts shadow
challenged from below by the clear
cut glass of a chandelier:
under this runs the hall,
drawing one deep into its recession
with a gleam on the floor-tiles,

and in the distance a flash
off conservatory windows
angled open to admit
a summer evening, the clip
of feet advancing, and a voice:
"I do not believe that you
have been here before," she says,
and though one has
what she says is true.

The Even Numbers

for Richard Verrall

The even numbers, as beautiful as vowels
   Emerging from the consonantal clasp
Of sounds that contain and yet unbind
   The o, the hidden aria, the bud
Unsheathing itself to flower on ear, on air—
   What would they do without the impaired, the odd
That show them for what they are?

If Bach had been a Beekeeper

If Bach had been a beekeeper
he would have heard
all those notes
suspended above one another
in the air of his ear
as the differentiated swarm returning
to the exact hive
and place in the hive,
topping up the cells
with the honey of C major,
food for the listening generations,
key to their comfort
and solace of their distress
as they return and return
to those counterpointed levels
of hovering wings where
movement is dance
and the air itself
a scented garden

Midwinter

Midwinter turning into twilight
    By the red farm: downpour drenches it,
A sore smear on a ground of green.
    A stream, surfeited with winter rain
Runs parallel to this hillside path
    As, far below, I sense suddenly
I am observed, sense before perception shows
    What eyes those are that follow me:
The stream is glancing skywards between trees
    That screen its banks, a thousand eye-whites
Divided by dark boles (their pupils),
    Each eye-white shared between two boles.
What I see's not real and yet is there—
    That endless stare goes on and on,
Eye after eye dogging my track.
    Turn back before darkness falls.
This I do, freed from that chain of eyes.
    The farm's owners have returned since I set out.

Their lights, extravagantly festive,
    Reveal the solidity of roughcast walls.
Twilight is kinder to their colour than the rain.
    The square flags of the barnyard are sleek with wet.
The new half-moon rides by with one straight side
    Cut out by shears.

February

In the month-long frost, the waters
    Combing the detritus that clogs a stream,
Leave gleaming in their wake these twists of glass,
    Caught crystals, petal and frozen frond:
At night, if you could fly and sweep
    With the owl's deep stare the valley reaches,
You would see in each waterway
    These barbed garlands glittering back
The light of an oval moon, whose full is failing,
    That must pull awry the brilliant symmetry of day
On freezing day, and leave to be melted at last
    These gauds that distract the owl's encompassing eye.

The Transformation

A morning moon
caught in the tree
begins its slide
slowly from branch to branch
behind the web
and tangled spokes of winter,
its midnight brilliance
made pale by daylight:
it is like seeing a face
grown suddenly old
that one had known
in all its youthful luminosity.

Ode to Memory

"Bird-witted"
is unjust—
call them all
winged memories: food
stowed and stored
to them means
food to be recalled:
they can trace months later
the where and when,
and what we would leave
forgotten, they will retrieve
in order of preference,
i.e., that which tastes best,
or should, if rot
has not decayed it: respect
the despised intellect
of birds, and when a name

out of the hundred that you know
refuses to appear
wish yourself bird-gifted,
and then go airily outside,
and on lifted wings
re-train the sights
of unfocused recollection, and if you can
become bird-brained.

The Leaper

Going from pool
to pool the moon
leaps on ahead of us,
always arriving
before we do, always
discovering how many
hollows the rain
had found to fill
along the mudslick path
that clings at the hill foot
to the level land,
and winds beside this stream
where the moon
must also be if only we
were wading it east
away from the going sun:
then we should see

on its surface
the continuous rippled moonface
replace the athlete moon
but cease to see
this invention of foot and eye
that moves because we
move, to tantalize
and lead us on
though it has never
shifted from being
that midsky beacon.

Fire and Air

Silk scarves of flame
wind from the coals
liquidly leaping them to and fro,
uncircling whichever way aircurrents go.

They aim to join
the airstream flowing above the house,
disordering every tree,
that lures them upwards into nonentity.

Strange, that opposites
should reach for the same
unassailable altitude
as if air and fire were a single flame.

As they are
when a house burns down
and they race the stairway, lit
by the one desire to have done with it,

leaving a silhouette
blackened behind them,
cardboard cut-out where once was wall,
swaying unflamelike, tottering to downfall.

A truce on the hearth tonight
keeps all in peace, in place,
mingling fire and air beyond blame.
Do not cease to admire such a scene. Do not trust a flame.

Primal Fire

This iridescent chaos
that assails the sense
each day—number
will never sway it.
Why did Plato dream
this stream might be canalised
by calling it illusion?
Trust to surfaces—
these are profundities:
you can neither drown
in them, nor outgaze
the maze of their intricacy.
They tell you who you are
and where—which is here,
between the sunlight
wakening on the wall
these variegated shadows
and the sun itself,
through days uncounted, unaccountable
pouring primal fire.

Watching Water

Why is it water, standing for itself,
   Runs to so many meanings? I watch
The flickerings, the flash, the out-and-through
   Past bridges, bank-side, flank
Of sand that rains have thickened to obstruct
   Its progress and have failed. The stream
That was brown and dark all day
   At evening takes-in the low light
Of yellow sundown and begins to brighten.
   The same stream where it flows through the wood
Seems to run over foil: its whisperings
   Fall then, splashing off the hillslope,
To tiny metallic crashes: it springs
   And bounds across the valley next,
Still swift, but fuller now, a bodied sound,
   Invitation to view the gathered present
Thing it is — watched water,
   Voicing a sinuous way near into far.

Floodtime

A thick-piled mat of foam
    Laps at a fallen trunk and then
Floats off in fragments, instantly renewed
    By the chafing forces from below
And the whip-lash blow on blow
    From a wind that suddenly will cease and then renew.
The millionaire looks to the lake he's made
    To show him himself as he would wish to be,
But it stretches today—all blind opacity—
    Across the grass it sucks at in frank greed,
As if licking it into life
    Not drowning out a separate existence.
Too full of itself, it pours off downhill
    To claim other acres, then joins the stream
That is river now and turns to watery morass
    Whatever it casts silt on,
The snakeshape current forcing a way inside
    The aperture of a bridge and getting through
By almost dragging the parapet after it,
    Repeating again and again this act
Of desolate possession, under a rain-choked sky,
    Waiting to end all here in blear not blaze,
In a world of water and as cold as stone.

The Martins

Like the particles of a bursting shell
    That nevertheless stay suspended
Moving together, a flock of martins
    Rising, prepare to ride the wind
Of their departure and their wings imagine
    The pull of it, anticipate the veerings
Against its mastery they must make their own.
    What they leave are eaves inhabited all summer
For the inhuman liberty of space:
    This is the trial, tomorrow they must go,
And in the empty nests another year
    Await its chances under clouds that steer
Rains across the mapped-out counties
    Above the migrating trickle of traffic moving.

Tonight

Tonight the sky stands cleansed
   Of all its trails save one that, slowly,
Before the dark comes on—dissolving
   From wrack to wraith—lets through
A high transparency. I wait beneath
   This no-man's territory to see
How far that fringe of vapour can prolong
   Its fading signature against space—
Space spreading upwards above shadow
   Whose steady seepage has now gained
The ground we are standing on. I grip
   With the eye that last dissolution in the sky
And pace the isthmus of the darkness under
   A solidity of trunks that wait to bear
The leaf-crowns of another year,
   Penetrating earth, preparing to drink light,
Upright across their tilted hemisphere.

Charles Tomlinson was born in Stoke-on-Trent, England, read English at Queens' College, Cambridge, and is the author of numerous volumes of poetry, literary essays, and admired translations, and editor of the important and acclaimed *Oxford Book of Verse in English Translation*. Mr. Tomlinson has received the Bennett Award from *The Hudson Review* for his achievement in poetry. He has also had shows in the United Kingdom of his paintings and drawings. He lives in England.

The New Criterion is recognized as one of the foremost contemporary venues for poetry with a regard for traditional meter and form. The magazine was thus an early leader in that poetic renaissance that has come to be called the New Formalism. Building upon its commitment to serious poetry, *The New Criterion* in 2000 established an annual prize, which carries an award of $3000. Charles Tomlinson is the third winner.